I Live Near a River

I Live Near a River

Text by Juliette Looye

Illustration: V. Jeffrey

Photography: © Michael T. Sedam/Corbis: cover; © Arend/Smith/ Alaskan Express/PictureQuest: detail, cover; © RubberBall Productions/PictureQuest: cover; © Michael T. Sedam/Corbis: detail, page 3; © Galen Rowell/Corbis: page 6; © DigitalVision/PictureQuest: page 7; © DigitalVision/PictureQuest: pages 10–11; © Troy Hunter: detail, page 11; © DigitalVision/PictureQuest: page 12; © David Muench/Corbis: page 13; © Corbis: pages 14–15; © RubberBall Productions/PictureQuest: page 14; © Alaska Stock/Alaskan Express/PictureQuest: detail, page 14

Literacy Consultant: Phoebe Bell Ingraham, Reading Recovery Teacher Leader, Wright State University

Literacy Teacher Advisors: Mona Bailey, Reading Specialist, Title I Coordinator; Amy Bodey, Reading Specialist; Samentha Lucas, Reading Specialist; Jessica McCombe, Reading Specialist

Reviewer: Kathryn A. Ebel, Ph.D., Geography Department, Ohio Wesleyan University

Developed by Kane Publishing Services, Inc., in cooperation with Zaner-Bloser, Inc.

ISBN: 0-7367-1932-6

Zaner-Bloser, Inc., P.O. Box 16764, Columbus, Ohio 43216-6764, 1-800-421-3018

Printed in China

03 04 05 06 07 (133) 5 4 3 2 1

Table of Contents

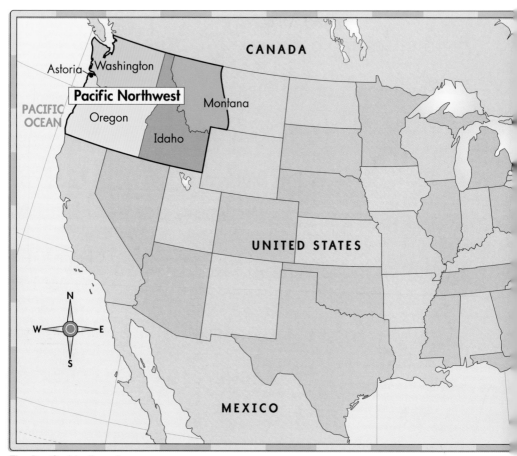

The Pacific Northwest

Patrick and His Home

Hello! I'm Patrick. I live in the city of Astoria, in the state of Oregon. I live in a part of the United States called the Pacific Northwest. The area got its name because it is in the northwest corner of the United States, and it is next to the Pacific Ocean.

The Pacific Northwest is made up of Oregon, Washington, Idaho, and western Montana. Here is a map of the United States. The Pacific Northwest is shown in color. Can you find the state of Oregon? The city of Astoria is marked on the map. Can you find Astoria, too?

The seaport in Astoria, Oregon

The city of Astoria is a **seaport**. That means that boats on the Pacific Ocean can sail right up to Astoria. Then the people on the boats can step onto the land. Here is a picture of the Port of Astoria. It is a busy place!

The Columbia River

My house is not far from the Columbia River. When I look out my bedroom window, I can see it. Have you ever seen one? Do you know what a river is? Have you ever been on or in one?

A **river** is a long body of water that flows through the land. Some rivers are small. They dry up during hot, dry weather and fill up again when it rains.

Some rivers are large. They are thousands of miles long. The Columbia River is a very large river. It is 1,243 miles long. It flows through Canada and the United States.

The Columbia River

The Mouth of the River

The part of the Columbia River that I can see from my window is called its **mouth**. You might think that a river's mouth is where it begins. But a river's mouth is where it *ends*. The Columbia River ends where it flows into the Pacific Ocean. So the Pacific Ocean is the Columbia's mouth.

Are you a little confused? If you are, think of it this way: When you let out a big breath, the air from your lungs moves out through your mouth and mixes with the air all around you. Well, the same thing happens with a river. The water from the Columbia River moves through its mouth and mixes with the water all around it. That water is the Pacific Ocean.

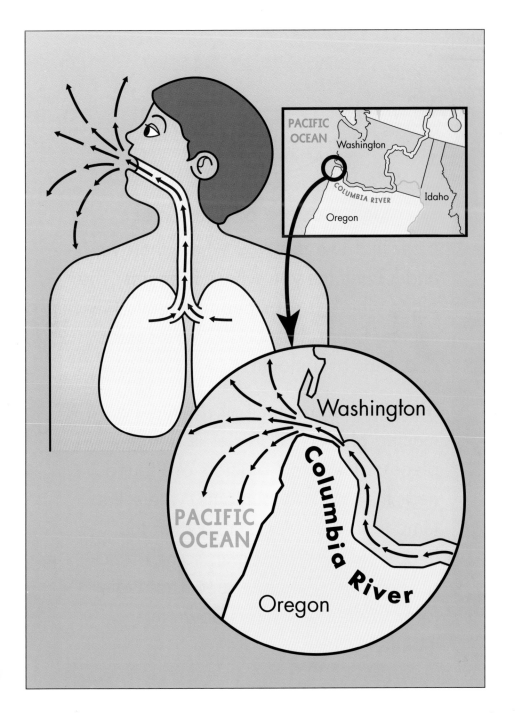

Washington

PACIFIC OCEAN

Columbia River

Oregon

PACIFIC OCEAN

Washington

COLUMBIA RIVER

Oregon

Idaho

9

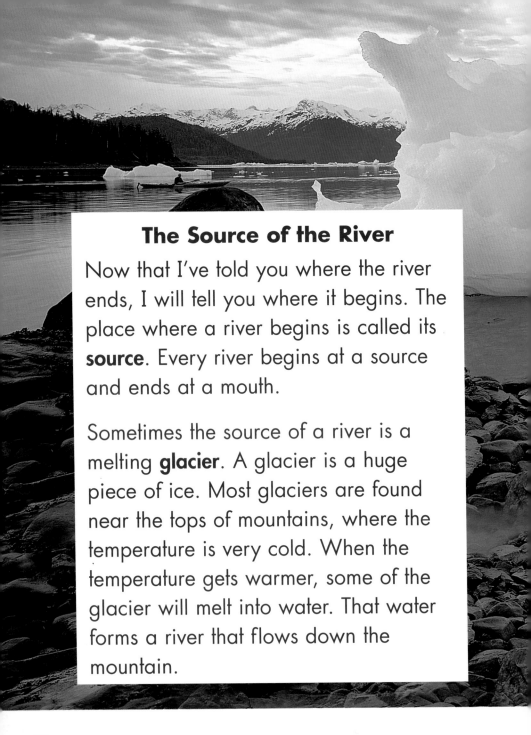

The Source of the River

Now that I've told you where the river ends, I will tell you where it begins. The place where a river begins is called its **source**. Every river begins at a source and ends at a mouth.

Sometimes the source of a river is a melting **glacier**. A glacier is a huge piece of ice. Most glaciers are found near the tops of mountains, where the temperature is very cold. When the temperature gets warmer, some of the glacier will melt into water. That water forms a river that flows down the mountain.

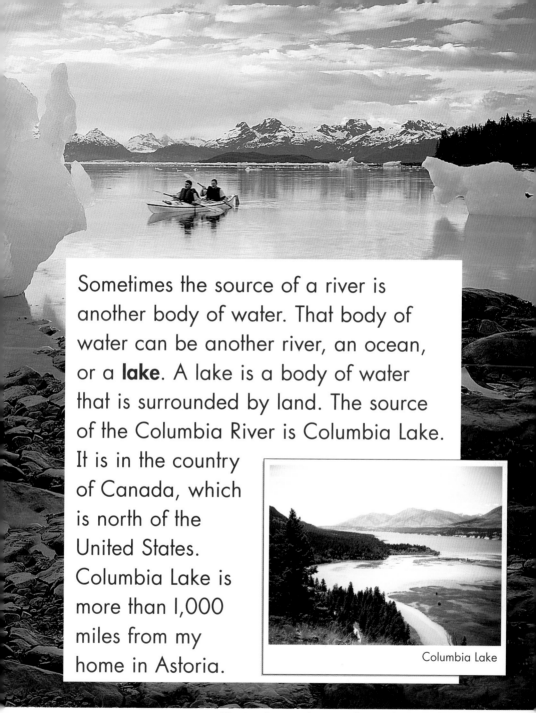

Sometimes the source of a river is another body of water. That body of water can be another river, an ocean, or a **lake**. A lake is a body of water that is surrounded by land. The source of the Columbia River is Columbia Lake. It is in the country of Canada, which is north of the United States. Columbia Lake is more than 1,000 miles from my home in Astoria.

Columbia Lake

The ice from a glacier melts and forms lakes and rivers.

The Course of the River

The part of a river between its source and its mouth is called its **course**. The map below shows the course of the Columbia River. As you can see, it doesn't flow in a straight line! The end of the river makes up much of the border between Washington and Oregon.

Many smaller rivers flow into the Columbia River. Those smaller rivers are called **tributaries**. The Columbia's largest tributary is the Snake River. It forms part of the border between Oregon and Idaho.

The Snake River

The Snake River runs through a huge **canyon** called Hells Canyon. It has very high sides and a flat bottom. It is made of volcanic rock. Like other canyons, it was formed by the river flowing through it and wearing away the rock. Hells Canyon is the deepest canyon in North America. In certain parts, it is almost 8,000 feet deep.

The Snake River in Hells Canyon

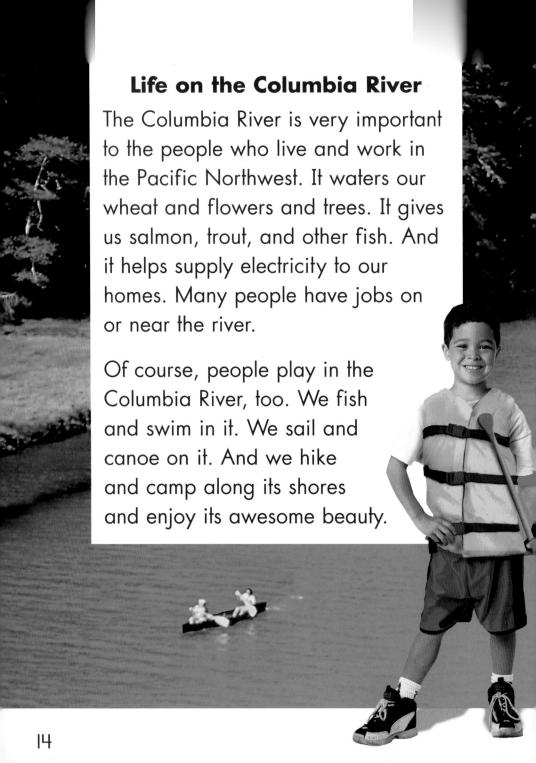

Life on the Columbia River

The Columbia River is very important to the people who live and work in the Pacific Northwest. It waters our wheat and flowers and trees. It gives us salmon, trout, and other fish. And it helps supply electricity to our homes. Many people have jobs on or near the river.

Of course, people play in the Columbia River, too. We fish and swim in it. We sail and canoe on it. And we hike and camp along its shores and enjoy its awesome beauty.

Glossary

canyon: a valley with very high sides and a flat bottom

course: the part of a river between its source and its mouth

glacier: a huge piece of ice, usually found at the top of a mountain

lake: a body of water that is surrounded by land

mouth: the place where a river ends and flows into a larger body of water

river: a long body of water that flows through the land

seaport: a city or town that boats can reach from the ocean

source: the place where a river begins

tributary: a river that flows into a larger river

Activity

Use the words from the list to answer these riddles about rivers.

course   **mouth**
tributary   **source**

1. I am the place where a river begins. I can be a glacier, a river, an ocean, or a lake. What am I?

2. I am the part of a river between its beginning and its end. I can flow for miles. What am I?

3. I am a river that flows into a larger river. What am I?

4. I am the place where a river ends. I flow into a larger body of water. What am I?